EMOTION

The Machinery of Life

The Missing Factors of Happy Relationships

Zsa Zsa Tudos

AKIA Publishing

First Edition
Published by AKIA Publishing
Copyright © *Zsa Zsa Tudos 2018*

The author asserts the moral right under the Copyright, Designs and Patents Act 1988 to be identified as the author of this work.

All Rights reserved. No part of this publication may be reproduced, stored in a retrieval system or transmitted, in any form or by any means without the prior consent of the author, nor be otherwise circulated in any form of binding or cover other than that which it is published and without a similar condition being imposed on the subsequent purchaser.

https://zsazsatudos.com
zsazsa@zsazsatudos.com

I dedicate this book to fellow earthlings who want to live happily ever after

It all happens in the mind

Content

1. As above — 13
2. So below — 17
3. Where do emotions come from? — 19
4. How can I understand more? — 25
5. Exercises — 37
6. Picture of the mind — 47
7. Your contribution to a relationship — 49
8. Common expressions — 51
9. Positive thinking — 59
10. Love — 61
11. Chemistry — 65
12. Attraction — 69
13. Layers — 71
14. Events to confront — 75
15. Depth of feelings — 81
16. Happiness is a state of mind — 85
17. Two individuals — 87
18. Togetherness — 89
19. Your partner is your new family — 91
20. Respect each other — 95

21. Learn your partner — 97
22. Relationship doesn't save your life — 101
23. Stock taking — 103

About myself

I am an educator, author and personal life coach. I have been teaching the mysteries of life and the universe, for over 30 years; have been a relationship and family counsellor for 20; also a personal life coach for the same time. I have 9 books published and working on a couple more at the moment.

I originate from the South of Hungary and currently living in London. I am saying currently because I lived in quite a few countries such as Greece, Spain, France and Brazil, and I taught in many more on the road of learning, experiencing and understanding. These aspects are vital to my teachings for whatever I teach, I experienced. I do not believe in academic learning unless strongly supported by practice.

You know every earthling has some kind of a call to follow. I consider myself to be on the quest of discovering solutions to the miseries of earthlings and make them understand that life is an extraordinary gift one needs to take on with curiosity and fire. On this path one can do but learn. I think of myself as an esoteric teacher in the purest sense. Esoteric is a Greek word meaning the highest knowledge that is only open for a small group of people. As you can see we use the word very loosely today. We call esoteric someone who lights a candle! It has nothing to do with it. It is a conscious and tiresome journey with amazing experiences.

I also want to add that there are no separate aspects of life, such as spirituality, finances, love life, personal life, family and so on. We have only one life within which everything is interrelated. Whatever and wherever you learn something, it could be readily used in every compartment. Learning is only good if you can put it into practice. Then it becomes Knowledge.

During my practice I realized that the biggest joy, and subsequently the biggest heartache of an earthling comes from human relationships. It is pretty logical for it is the only interactive communication we experience.

Until today I was engaged in personal, live teaching for small selected groups. Momentary I have a few handfuls of students in various countries, some of them have been with me for 20 years! They are really beyond everyday understanding! And they are still learning!

My students greatly benefitted from my teachings. They understand the matrix of the universe and their place in it, they love themselves, they learned to make choices, they are open to experiences and new events, and they have aims and really good relationships. They also know how to heal, help aims to get on the right track and benefit from all the so called gifts given to earthlings.

So I came up with solutions for books and online webinars, keeping in mind that life is short and we should make the most of it.

I am hoping for many readers and students who value themselves enough to start learning how to value The Self and Life with it.

Live in the present!

FOREWORD

Dedicate a notebook to your relationship readings and studies and jot down your questions, answers, thoughts, to make them conscious. I know we have gadgets to do it for us and sound recognition, but unless you use your hand and a pen to form the letters you are not going to get there.

I also organized this book a bit like an exercise book. I gave you questions to think about and I left some space for you to use while reading. This arrangement will allow you to read and take notes easily during travelling. However, use your dedicated journal for extended writings.

I am planning a series of *Emotions* books. This one highlights the common mistakes people make when they decide to enter into or stay away from a romantic relationship. The next will be about actual dating and sexuality and the third will be about forming a family and inviting children. I also plan to write about spiritual couplehood and spiritual parenting.

Please note: my books are non-religious and non-racist. My teachings are about earthlings and their emotions as human beings.

1.

As above

The Universe is an ever-expanding and constantly moving energy mass. This motion is provided by the interactions of individual units. On the big scale, there are galaxies formed around a strong magnetic centre. The strength of the galaxy depends on the volume of the pulling and pushing power. Since similar energies like each other, Solar Systems within need to agree with the Core. Translating it to energy, they have to resonate on the same or fairly similar level, or push the Core towards their liking. The higher the resonance the better the quality and faster the energy. However, it is axiomatic that after reaching a certain height, the only direction is to go down. There are two choices to go to. Narrow-minded energies proceed forward without noticing the warning signs, give up their individuality and amalgamate with the centre. This centripetal motion stops the pushing and pulling power and the galaxy disappears as a functioning unit. The other road is expanding. This is the *spreading the knowledge* road. High resonance can only be achieved by experience that adds to the knowledge of the unit. The phenomena force the planets of the galaxy to leave the base and look for experiences elsewhere. This centrifugal motion releases the unit and allows it to find a new place. A planet cannot and do not wander around; it is not possible since some kind of attraction has to hold it in place. Therefore the easiest choice is the neighbouring galaxy. The same law is true for those with low frequency, slow energy. Whatever happens, a galaxy needs constant pushing and pulling power to survive. Otherwise, it falls into the abyss.

There were clever people before me, such as Hermes Trismegistos, to state: *as above so below.* If you think of it, I have just described human relationships and the individuals in it. It is even truer for romantic involvements.

The biggest pitfall of earthlings is that they cannot see. They are reluctant to enter into the process of evolving. They like to follow routines and stay within the comfort zone. Nevertheless, they do not want to be alone for it is a given that should not. Therefore they take someone into their microcosm with a desire to continue living on the same note. Otherwise, they put the heavy responsibility for a better life on the shoulders of the newcomer. Either way, the pushing - pulling motion is not their favourite philosophy for living. However, without it, the relationship disappears, and the individuals concerned would give up their lives to circle the consciously or subconsciously chosen centre. In the minds of earthlings, these phenomena exist as a picture for the most perfect couplehood. In this picture two lonely, abandoned and incomplete halves find each other and make up the perfect one. The first question that comes to mind would be: why do we call it couplehood if there is only one in it? Or relationship, as the matter of fact. In a healthy togetherness, there are two complete individuals, who put their power together and support each other on the road to achieving the dreams they set out to reach. Naturally, a relationship would put responsibilities on the shoulders of both persons equally to maintain the evolution of the couplehood also. The relationship and individuality need to co-exist. I cannot really say in peace, for peace is quiet and emotionless, hence the vital motion for proceeding would be lacking. People have different approaches to convincing and it often falls into a fierce argument. On this note, an understanding is required. An argument is an exchange of thoughts. If you want to convince your partner of the legitimacy of your idea, be ready to see the other side of the road also. The key is respect. There is always a leader in a togetherness, it has to be. However, the leadership shifts from time to time or events to events.

Penny for your thoughts:

2.

So below

I would like to go back to the mentioned energies. When I say energy I talk about interacting physically measurable substances. They have frequency, speed, colour, smell, substance, taste and sound. These qualities make up the value of certain energy. If you think about it, these characteristics are all valid for human beings also.

I put energies into two main categories: organic and non-organic. The best way to differentiate is to understand that organic energies are capable of physical changes, such as growing, reproduction and recuperating from inflicted wounds. All non-organic energies were organic at some point for everything comes from organic materials of the planet. However, earthlings are destroyers. Organic energies of natural substances were manipulated into synthetic material in order to withstand time and weather conditions. Nevertheless, motion, provided by the pulling-pushing powers is in everything. In non-organic energies, the movement is much slower, just enough to keep the mass together.

This little introduction of the macrocosm will prove very useful later.

Penny for your thoughts:

3.

Where do emotions come from?

The life-giving and saving motion of energies derive from the interrelations of emotions.

Emotions are the machinery of life. Without them, organic energies would not survive.

I remember one day sitting in a garden restaurant in Budapest, sipping wheat beer with my students and their colleagues from work, when one started to talk about his relationship, putting emphasis on his abrupt behaviour towards the girlfriend. I knew he was fishing for some professional advice that I am always very happy to give when having fun. I asked him what the trigger of his conduct was. He said he did not know. It just came from nowhere. When I asked him to classify where nowhere was, he motioned to the air around us. I looked at him perplexed. He was an engineer who worked with numbers and facts, even though he was comfortable saying that. Then I told him that nowhere is somewhere, otherwise, it wouldn't exist. And if it doesn't exist, nothing can come from there. Not even emotions. Now, I became the centre of confused glances. But after a short silence, they all started to smile and reassured me that I was right.

If you think about it, we are very comfortable with a certain explanation. We take them on board without giving them a thought. However, everything is logical in life and happens for a reason. Nothing comes from nowhere! Nowhere doesn't exist.

Emotion is the motion of thoughts and thoughts are the mirrors of understanding. It is not very strange really for who you are and what you do, reflect your mental grab of what you know. Knowing is very tricky. We use the word the same way we live; without thinking about its meaning. Knowing means that you understand something fully, within the interrelations of events. Knowing is experiencing and learning from it. The danger of using this word lies in believing to be accurate. I would not say true as that is another word for the mirror. There is no such thing on Earth we can call truth. Or yes but then we need to take it on board with a pinch of salt. Everybody's truth about the same event is different. Let me give you an example: I love Mexico. I visited the country on a number of occasions. For years I have been thinking of moving there for people are nice, the food is good, the weather is excellent and the whole Mayan approach is peaceful. However, when I mentioned my last trip to people they looked at me perplexed, some even with a hint of disgust. When I ask questions, none of them can come up with any kind of experience there. They mention drugs, but aren't they everywhere? They did a survey and measured the cocaine substance in the air of Madrid and it topped the chart. Even the US comes long before Mexico in drug consumption! They also say there is a danger that comes from the mentioned problem. Again, isn't it everywhere? Most killings in Spain are drug-related, but the media doesn't connect the two and not announcing the country as dangerous. People are very happy to take their dream holidays on the Costas without giving it another thought. One of my sisters lives in Canada and she said that she would not go to Mexico because they kill Canadians. Wow, these Mexicans are pretty clever people! How do they know who is Canadian? It is not an ethnic group, anybody could be taken for a citizen of the country. You see, people just follow ideas, the mind manipulation of the media and imagination, supported by their fear of the unknown. Believe me, it is an extraordinary place that I had the privilege of visiting on more than one occasion before.

In this story which viewpoint is true? Both of them or you might say none. And since the media gives you plenty of advice on relationship issues, you really need to start thinking and find real values behind the mass consciousness.

My story also serves as an example of emotion altering and mind manipulation. The more you know and understand the less manipulated you are.

I do not get into the details of what it is you need to understand because it is everything. It is the whole existence, your family, friends, how to work, behave, dress, treat yourself and do certain chores. Life is an evolution of the mind and emotions.

Penny for your thoughts:

Affirmation

I clear my thoughts of all

misconceptions

4.

How can I understand more?

First of all, you need to learn to use all your senses. Since they deemed the method the most clear-headed and emotionless, today's earthlings make their decisions almost solely on what they see. The argument is that there are no surprises and hidden issues there. This way of thinking is very dangerous. None of what you see is emotionless. And as such, it cannot be clear-headed. Then again, your clear head and rational understanding are governed by your view of the issue involved. And your view is created by your understanding. Isn't it fun?

I would also like to remind you of the most important quote from *The Little Prince* a book by *Antoine de Saint-Exupery*: "One sees clearly only with the heart. The essential is invisible to the eye."

The eye is a very interesting tool. In reality, you not see what is there but catch the light reflected from the object or subject. Even though you only see what you allow yourself to do so. It means that you filter the images by your conscious and subconscious. At this moment we may translate them as mental and emotional for the sake of simplifying the happening. It is also vital to realize that we only focus on one eye at a time. The brain selects the eye according to the information within, and the opinion, even if we consciously haven't formed any.

- Let us do an exercise. Put your palm in front of the left eye to make sure that you focus on the right. Look at the subject of your desire and jot down the thoughts entering your mind. You might even see colours. Make note of everything you sense. After change eyes and now focus on the left. Again write everything down there. You will notice that the two impulses are different. You would associate one picture with the heart and the other one with the mind. It is also interesting to note that when you are angry with the beloved person, your emotions would blend into the picture. You see your subject in a different light altogether. It happens because that is what you want to see.

Since I am a woman, I will usually use *him* for the person in the story. However, gender doesn't matter in most cases.

Every experience you have reflects your momentary feelings even if they are not related to the event. When you are sad, the whole world looks blue; when you are joyful, pink becomes your colour. By nature earthlings belong to either of these 2 categories: 1. the glass is half empty and 2. the glass is half full. These are two opposite observations of the same view or idea. You might want to argue that both mean half a glass of something. Sure! However, the first comment emphasises what is absent, while the second considers the existing amount more important.

- Which one is yours? Why did you choose that particular group? Write your answer down in your journal.

Translating the idea to relationship and emotions within, I would say that the first case shows people with expectations and concealed emotions. If you belong to this group you put conditions on feelings and would never be able to open up completely unless you switch views. Looking at the missing factors puts weight on dissatisfaction. It could be rewarding if advances are planned and executed by the Self. However, it is common to expect others to fill the gaps. It means that nothing is good for you and the whole world is responsible for the situation. The danger is that people with *discontentment syndrome* very rarely arrive at the point we commonly call happiness, for they are constantly missing something. These people cannot handle disappointments so they are always unsatisfied. What is a disappointment? It is an undesired result of events with choices. Why are you disappointed? Due to the unfulfilled expectations. And what are expectations? They are your limited understanding of life, within which you are aiming for the best result. However you refuse to step out of your comfort zone, I usually refer to as the microcosm, and you do not really want to work on the issue. Expectations are reflecting your fears or very often, your lack of motivation. It is far easier to belong to this category. You do nothing, you expect. And you can always moan about it to the world! Tell others that your life is unlucky. All the misery only happen to you. You require hugs and reassurance that people around you feel your pain. It is really crazy! On top of not helping yourself, you bring the surrounding down to your level. Well, it has to be done, for similar energies like each other, and if those in your immediate vicinity maintain the faster energy, you might have to climb out of your pit to meet them. That is something you do not consider so you do the best you can to take them with you. As an illusion, it feels busy for you are running up and down to look for the missing parts. This movement provides you with the essential drive you need for a living but it doesn't take you anywhere. You are just moving in circles, chasing your tail so to speak.

The second group of earthlings is those who continuously look at the sunny side of the road.

Whatever happens around them the Sun would never stop beaming. If you belong to this category you do not want or cannot handle disappointments. That is why you are always satisfied. Does it sound familiar? Most certainly! It is the other side of the road! The mirror of the same emotion we have just talked about. When the Sun is always shining you have the illusion that there is nothing else to do anymore. Everything is honky dory as English people would say. You sit down and gaze into the world with satisfaction. These people usually do not have aims for they are afraid of rejection and failure. It is silent and motionless vegetating. For the physical body, it might be better due to the lack of stress so the nerve system remains fairly untouched. However, evolution, learning, and changing are not on the plate for these earthlings.

If you want to see events clearly you need to understand both sides of the road. One cannot be appreciated without the other. You only enjoy light if you see dark. Light doesn't make sense without dark. And vice versa. You should not be afraid of experiencing emotions.

In everyday speaking, and even written materials some people consider calling the behaviour of these groups positive and negative. I detest these terms for they do not make sense to me! Positive and negative are the opposite physical polarities of an energy mass. They are neither good nor bad. I also noticed that people used them as synonyms for good and bad. It is even more disturbing. Good and bad are relative terms on their own right, making just as little sense and the other two.

As I mentioned earlier positive and negative are polarities. They do not carry quality values for they represent the two opposite poles in everything. They co-exist within, never interchanging but preserving life by pushing and pulling each other. Their unique characteristic is that whatever happens, by nature they only go forward. Good and bad on the other hand describe qualities observed by a particular being and judged according to his understanding. A good for someone is always bad for someone else who looks at the event differently. It doesn't make one of the persons a good one and bad the other. They are only different.

There are no good people or bad people. Some might be nearer to the mass consciousness but the quality of this brainwashing movement was set by people, who decided upon certain rules to cushion their comfort zone. You might say that yes, but what about killers? Interesting question. There are masses of unlawful killings going on in the world and all of them are applauded by certain groups and it doesn't enter your mind to call them killers in case you belong to any of the groups. You see, it depends on your standpoint. And your standpoint is formed by your education, background, beliefs and the media as the base. Your individual experiences will be added to this foundation. It is like building a house. The stronger the foundation the more difficult it is to alter the style of the house. A gothic groundwork would not take on an art nouveau building light-heartedly. You may ignore your change in the approach and use the solid base anyway, but believe me, it will come back and haunt you as long as you exist. Look back in history. Earthlings have been using the, *what one cannot see is not there,* policy by demolishing buildings, wipe them off the ground and replace them with something totally different in value. Funnily most of these actions were noted as a victory by the destroyers. However, without digging the roots out, a tree would start growing when the weather conditions are adequate. In case you wonder about the meaning of this example, I tell you now.

We think that couplehood is formed by two persons who agree to spend the rest of their lives together in some kind of agreement on important issues and have amazing sexual encounters. Sure! However, the joining parties come from somewhere and they carry a package. I could call every matrimony a package deal. However, I want you to understand that they should not be. Coming from a strong family would lend you the feeling of security and the reassurance that everything will be all right if you continue with the rules you learned as a child. Nevertheless, your partner comes with another set of important rules and in most cases, they are totally different from those you have in your backpack. The newlyweds, with or without papers pledging their union, start wrestling at the moment of moving in. As they do, families have this strange idea that they are all invited to take part and voice their opinion in the event. Now you can see why the great majority of unions break up due to families of the couple involved. It is a power struggle where innocent people get hurt and nobody cares. I am not saying you should abandon the family you grew up in. However, you need to be strong enough and form opinions independently within your relationship. Struggles should be solved within. Asking opinions of people around would be seen as an invitation to *move in.* As they start judging your partner and you, your life and attitude, so they alter your thoughts. Judging is the biggest mistake in relationships. You either do it out of fear or you are convinced that you hold the truth in your head and heart. If you think about it, the latter is a narrow-minded approach to living together or couplehood. Earthlings are not robots. They are constantly forming and shaping through effects, even if they do not want. The direction of the journey is chosen by the individual. It might be a subconscious favouring but it still is.

Some kind of inclination is present in everybody in the form of life philosophy. The way one looks at life could be shallow or deep, simple or complicated, stagnant or ever-changing, as the result of the individual view built on information collected and processed. So as you see life is a chain of events, created by thoughts and emotions to give fuel to the machinery.

- Do you have a life philosophy?
- What are your aims?

Penny for your thoughts:

Affirmation

I allow my emotions to flow

5.

Exercises

I am sure we can agree that everything we do, how we see and how we carry ourselves, depend on momentary or hopefully only semi-permanent feelings we created.

Let us do a few exercises. I would like you to think about the following questions and write your answers down in the journal you created when you started to read the book. It is necessary to be as honest as possible. Dig deep down into your thoughts and feelings. Be specific! Write at least ten sentences.

- How do I see my perfect partner?

Consciously you want the, *live happily ever after*, scenario. You keep nurturing an image in your mind about the beginning of *real life*. What is in this picture? And that is the problem. You see it like a picture! And pictures are static. They do not move and they do not live. They are dead! They capture a certain moment of life, usually arranged for your wish. If you have a crush you try to organize events to have the two of you near enough to each other to take a photo. Today it is easy. You just fiddle with your phone and hoppaaaa, there is a picture. Or invite Photoshop to help you. In some cases, it could work out initially. Joining two people together on a photo strengthen the chance of the two of them meeting. Nevertheless, I need to warn you that it is Witchcraft, for it is a conscious manipulation of energies. Of course, we use the art every day, only we do not understand it. Perhaps you want to familiarize yourself with the Royal Art. My webinars on the subject will be available on akialight.com.

Let us get back to pictures and the thoughts in your mind. In the consumerist society where most of us live, we have been led to believe that what we see is what we get. We buy things for the package. We look for the packaging. Big money is spent on certain brands, only because they are announced fashionable by the media. An event comes to my mind associated with this behaviour. A friend and her friend came to visit me. We walked around in the fashionable district of the city, window-shopping and chatting about non-important issues. Suddenly the friend disappeared into a posh bag shop I would think twice to enter. When he came out, after a long wait, he carried a simple, black shoulder bag. I looked at him confused. I could not figure out how was it possible to get this particular bag in that shop. He noticed my face and announced that it was a famous brand and cost him €620 (US$760) with a 20% discount as a returning customer. Then I opened my eyes even wider. I had this urge to touch this treasure. And can you believe it? It wasn't even leather! However, there was a small silver plate on it with a fashionable brand name. I am not saying you shouldn't imagine someone fashionable to cross your path. I am not even saying that it is bad behaviour to spend on labels. I am only saying that you need to look deeper than the packaging.

Think about it! The partner you want would be outstanding in every way. A face and body to be proud of, a socializing wizard with an amazing sense of humour, someone who makes enough money to dismiss worries concerning the material welfare of a unity, kind and attentive, always ready to help and jump in whenever and wherever needed. On top of all he would never look at anybody else but the one and only, the chosen love of his life. He would learn new tricks every day to please you and bring joy into your life. On the other hand, the chosen girl would naturally look like a carefully made-up model, well-dressed, lively, but only with you, with a good career aspect, a good housewife, but not neglected, an amazing lover and cater for your needs in every way. Most of all you want someone who makes your friends immensely jealous and would please your mother first of all.

These fantasies are only brushing the surface. You do not want a human being, you want a robot. Do not forget you are not your mother and you cannot please everybody.

We will talk about the soul's journey and soul relations within a family in another publication.

Parents are people who have the opportunity to put into practice all that they learned and also gain experiences through parenting. It is the only time when earthlings subconsciously invite a newcomer into their comfort zone, never realizing and never understanding the consequences. That is why most relationships shake after having children. This is the time when every relationship needs a coach to help reorganize emotions, thoughts, powers, and importance.

Even though Andersen, Grimm, and Disney are reassuring you that you only need to get to the long white dress and the tuxedo, and the gate of, *live happily ever after,* will open, and real togetherness only starts at that point. I am not saying that you do not need a registration of unity. It can be unregistered quite easily. However, some kind of a ceremony, even if only the two of you are taking part in it, is important to mark the sincerity of the commitment.

You need to elaborate and personalize rather than having general ideas. Do not look at a static picture! Life is in constant motion and your desire is a human being who goes through events and has to make choices from time to time. It is important, for general ideas have almost nothing to do with your personal choices. Use all the five senses and describe his fragrance, the feeling in your fingertips when you touch him, the picture you see when you look at him, the sound you hear when you say his name and the taste of his kiss.

When you finished, close your eyes and go through a day together that you would deem perfect. Keep in mind that life is moving and there are families, friends, and people around.

- The next step is to imagine the two of you in five years.

Has anything changed? I sincerely hope so! Reflecting your thoughts on life and the future, you would trigger certain emotions, when faced with this hypothetical question. If you are a half-empty person you would have a bleak outcome, despite your desire for a rosy one. However, if you are a half-full person would get a static image with the two of you with two children in front of a nice yard. All of you are neatly dressed and well-behaved.

- What happens in 10 years?

Everybody enters into or should enter into a relationship with a thought of forever in mind. Otherwise, it is not worth it. Ten years sounds like forever at the beginning or as a future image of something non-existent just yet. Therefore this picture would look very similar to all. A decade yields success that even the most suspicious mind would acknowledge.

- How do you imagine a relationship?

Again you learn to elaborate and personalize. Compare the idea of the perfect partner with the one in the perfect relationship. Do they match?

- What do I think of my parents as people?

This question produces mixed feelings in people. In our minds parents are not people. They belong to a special race with obligation and hardship to further the lives of their creations. We never look at them as lovers, really they have no time for that anyway and they are too old!

It might sound unorthodox what I am about to say. Please do not dismiss it without thinking about it.

First, you are a lover, second, you are a partner and third, you are a parent.

Either we like it or not sexuality is the basic feature of a romantic relationship. Mixing up these priorities would result in a bleak and pressurized existence. The solution to every problem within hides in sexuality regardless of the background, age or religion. Even if you consider your mother-in-law being the troublemaker.

When I mention sex or sexuality I do not mean intercourse. I mean Life, I mean Creation, I mean Sparkles in the air, I mean Exciting Togetherness. I mean the strength of support you offer each other and the view that He is a God and She is a Goddess. It is total trust and respect.

- Do you dare to look at your parents as an outsider?

The greatest influence, apart from the mass media, comes from our parents. Although they do the best they can, nobody is born to be a parent. They are people who do parenting according to their understanding. They have a double standard to live up to couplehood and parenting.

Penny for your thoughts:

Affirmation

I am a lover first

6.

Pictures of the mind

Pictures of the mind can be misleading. If there is an ex you feel particularly nostalgic about, you are going to look at pictures where the two of you are holding hands, kissing and usually nobody is around. But you cannot hold hands all the time, your lips would get tired of kissing and people live around you. There is always a girlfriend who is envious of your sudden fortune of having somebody, a friend who is more sensitive or comforting than you are and happy to jump in, parents who would say: *we want the best for you darling, he is no good for you* or *my beautiful son, she cannot take care of you as well as I can and so on.* These are thoughts of selfish narrow mindedness when parents are afraid of changes in their little bubble and to lose control of their creations, meaning you. Mistakenly these actions are taken for love and caring.

- Do you have a picture? What is on it?

Affirmation

My partner is my new family

7.

Your contribution to a relationship

We call it a couplehood, for two persons are interacting, in the hope of richer fulfilment. Or at least it should be the case. Exes of any kind should be left behind, questions answered and emotional traumas dealt with. Bringing your previous relationship into your new one is disrespectful towards your new partner and also yourself. It is your responsibility to deal with your past on your own or with the help of a professional but not your future.

It is also important to start something new wholeheartedly rather than *let's see* attitude.

I would like you to look into yourself, dig deep down and find all the wonderful things you would contribute to your relationship. Do not be afraid to contribute! Some people say that it is better to be loved than love. They also advise not to give yourself away and do not show emotions. There are thousands of books talking about dating rules and body language. I've just learned that many earthlings pay good money for webinars on the subject! Guys, you need to understand something! We are not dealing with robots! Every human being is different in every situation. One who appears calm with you might get frustrated with another person. This is the law of attraction! The interrelation of energies! So you need to work on your couplehood. Not on your partner! It seems to be the inbuilt idea of earthlings to turn the other person into a *clone!* Can you imagine to sit with yourself and be with yourself throughout the years! It is outright crazy!

Be generous! Give and learn to receive!

Penny for your thoughts:

8.

Common expressions

- **Miracles**

The world is full of, so-called optimists and know it all-s, who believe in affirmations and again, so called positive way of thinking; also, that important events in life are destined. Tons of workshops, lectures, talks, and books are there to give you sound advice about successful behaviour patterns, what to wear, what to say, how to carry yourself and put yourself out there, in order to enter into the Nirvana of a relationship. Some tell you to write affirmations on the mirror, the wall and say them every morning. Others would suggest having a miracle box at your door, with your written wishes, to bring into your place what your heart desires. Besides, all say that you need to believe in love. However you do not understand what love is, miracles are illusions, fantasies or hopes that feed on the lack of information. It is something that you do not understand and usually attribute to a supernatural power or fate. However, in life, only a few events are outlined. Even then, you have the liberty of declining or accepting them.

Do not forget, that for a new-born everything is a miracle. Due to the lack of information, a baby doesn't question anything; as a sponge, it takes in the wonders around. But you are an adult and according to your curiosity and intelligence, you have collected data on your way. So use this data to ask questions. For example: who is in charge of miracles? Where does he/she/it live? How miracles are made? Well, if they are made, they are not miracles, for somebody can make them. In this case, it is only a miracle for you because you do not understand how it is done.

It doesn't mean that you should not picture your future in your mind. It only means that you have to work on it. Without conscious work, you will never get there. Even Cinderella went to the ball! And either consciously or subconsciously she lost her slipper when the prince was running after her.

This story is a great example of human behaviour. Do not forget that all fairy tales are written by earthling and it is also important to understand that the authors of the classics are males. In every fairy tale, the male is a hunter who goes through difficulties to reach the subject of their desire. Females, like Cinderella, conveniently lose their slippers to draw the track for the hunting.

- **Destiny**

What is destiny? Well, it is very easy to clarify the meaning of destiny. It is to be at the right place at the right time. However, there is a misunderstanding about destiny. Earthlings usually think that it is written somewhere and against all odds, it has to happen.

Due to the interrelations of energies and the fact that similar energies like each other – this is the meaning of the law of attraction – there are events that would be more likely to happen than others. However, the likelihood depends on the individuals concerned. In one's life, there are always choices to make. The more choices you allow yourself the bigger are the chances that you meet someone. Following a routine diminishes your attention to details and you would aim for the destination rather than enjoy the ride. From time to time you need to follow your intuitions. I do not say always because one has to learn about intuitions, and how to distinguish thoughts of the mind and choices given from the universe. You also need flexibility in your aims. As an example: you decide to study because everybody is pushing you and due to the nature of the family business your choice would fall on chemistry. However on the road, you realize that you dislike it or you do not have the discipline, the study would require. So you have to make some adjustments to your aim of studying. The greater aim is still there but the road would be different because you changed your approach and instead of equations of chemical substances you will be looking at fabrics and the latest issue of Vogue for your fashion designer aim. It makes you happy and you become a hot name on the market. We could call it destiny because you had the urge to study! You were brave enough to alter the route. You might not be able to join the firm but you find something you are excited about and able to pursue. It is the same with every choice. If the aim is to get bread you might want to choose a different route to the bakery! To see something new, to meet someone new. You might even discover that there is a new bakery opened recently and sells much better bread than the one you usually go to. And there is a very charming person working there, or buying a sandwich! So you see, you make your destiny! You make your destiny by being open-minded and not afraid of changes.

- **Soulmates**

They do exist. Soulmates have the same soul number as you. It means that you are from the same soul family.

I do not want to get into the evolution of a soul here because it would cause havoc. Perhaps we will talk about it in another webinar here.

Like many other important phrases, a soulmate is used without real meaning today. Within this meaning, there is a big controversy. We say that a soulmate is somebody who understands you, who is able to finish your sentences, who knows what you are thinking and with whom you feel comfortable. Are you thinking what I am? How do you call it a relationship when there is only you in it? What about the other person? Oh yes, the other person is the admirer! And you are admired! This kind of arrangement is the easy way out and doesn't take you anywhere. It is static.

We usually meet soulmates for important teachings or events in life for we help each other to learn, to evolve and to find the road towards happiness. As you can figure from what I was saying, we have many soulmates and only a few of them are for romantic involvement. But not only one. Like everything, it is good and bad. Good, because you have choices and bad because you can never be certain that the choice you made is the best one. I want to reassure you, that whatever choice you make, is the best one at the time. Keep in mind that we put out 100% of our capabilities at every given moment. So we should not regret but explore the possibilities.

Every 100% is related to the momentary circumstances, mental and emotional welfare of the particular individual. The journey of life is designed for individuals who interact with others and might decide to walk the path together and help, monitor and teach each other.

Every soulmate is good for a romantic relationship at a certain time of your life, and it is true for him/her also. But you might not meet at that time. Apart from that, we have soul mates of both sexes and your sexual preference plays an important role here.

- **Twinflames**

Twinflame we have only one in the whole universe. That is why we call it a twin-flame. Your twin flame is literary the other half of you. Oh, I know, now you are getting hopeful! So there is a One and Only! Yes. But this, one and only, is so comfortable to be with that romance is almost out of the question. As if you have been with yourself. Romance and sexuality need fire and lust and we usually do not lust after ourselves. And do not forget, we are here on Earth to learn and evolve. In the comfort zone, there is nothing to learn. Twinflames are dead-end streets with limited possibilities.

Perhaps I add a few more thoughts. I did not want to get into esoteric knowledge here but I have no choice. The fashionable media picks up certain expressions, like twin flames and gives them to you with the importance they created. This expression comes from a deep knowledge of esoteric wisdom. The funny and sad part is that nobody questions the origin of the word only starts running and searching for the twin flame. I give you a very short explanation here.

When a soul reaches the highest level of evolution it divides into two. Just like the water drop; as it is filled, there is a time when one drop cannot hold the water segments together and divides into two drops, marking the beginning of two independent lives. So your twin flame is actually you.

9.

Positive thinking

I must admit, I am still confused about the meaning of this expression, for positive is a physical polarity. Does it mean good or optimistic? However good doesn't exist really, for it mirrors the momentary situation of a certain point of view. Even the momentary good for one person would be bad for another one. Let us stay with a relationship. If your crush decides to be with you, I am sure somebody is crying over the happening. Positive thinking definitely doesn't mean good.

So it has to be optimistic. But what is optimistic? Do you say the sun is shining when it rains? You convince yourself that you are all right when you are not? Do you say you are happy when you are very far from it? It is a slight alteration on the soulmate issue. You are convincing yourself that everything is honky dory so there is nothing to be done. You are convincing yourself that dreams would happen by themselves and you can sit your life through, everything will come to you by thinking about it.

However, this attitude only works if it is accompanied by action; without it, we arrive back to the miracle box and the so-called secret. Believe me, these are the biggest illusions of all. A person who has no funds, no dying wealthy relatives to inherit from, and no lottery ticket whatsoever, but dreams about the latest Ferrari, would never arrive there, despite the power of thoughts. In Africa millions of people starving to death daily, and I am certain that their desire for food is stronger than anything; nevertheless, the heavens do not open, and roast chicken will not fall from the sky. Yes, strong thoughts would bring a better result. However, it is not a miracle but the manipulation of energies and that is the gift of humanity. One should not do anything without total commitment so if you are looking for a relationship you should believe in the result and do something about it! You see, even Cinderella went to the ball!

10.

Love

There are two common understandings of the meaning of love. The first says that love is unconditional and the second announces that it is heavily conditioned. These are the 2 ends of the scale. And the truth is travelling in between.

Out of the many types of love now we talk about romantic love; living-together love.

What is love? Is it an emotion? Is it a state of mind? Is it a state of life? If it is an emotion, what kind of feelings associated with it? Joyous, bitter, sweet, fiery, lusting, forgiving, jealous, envious, sad, angry? If you think about it, the love we usually understand would entail all these feelings. Just as life would. It is an adventurous, trying and teaching association with the Self. The other person in the relationship is the mirror. By looking at the mirror you see yourself.

It is also fashionable to say that love is unconditional. So is life. But do we understand what unconditional means? It means that there are no "only ifs" in life and love.

If love is unconditional it is neutral and emotionless. For we cannot get angry if our feelings are not reciprocated or the chosen person doesn't follow the rules and regulations we set out. And we cannot love the subject more if we are pleased with the actions taken.

On the other hand, as the opposite pole, love is the collective name for all the feelings possible. It is an angry-joyous and sweet-bitter existence with great manipulating and healing power. It is life itself. As with all aspects of life, it is up to the individual to play the scale between the 2 poles. Your attitude towards love and relationships would be filtered by your mind, the conscious and subconscious.

However we are not after the love available through human relationship, but chasing a dream of constant ecstasy or peace and quiet, with an assurance of forever. Well, this ecstasy business is confusing for us. Subconsciously we are for continuous changes. The reason is, that everything is in motion in the universe and this movement is the fuel of Life. Without it, the whole universe would cease. Can you imagine? If Earth stopped turning and travelling around the Sun, and all the other planets stood still, they would fall apart because there would not be pulling and pushing power, in one word, interrelation. We are part of the Universe and we work the same way. In the case of Earthlings, this power mainly comes from emotions. And since we cultivate our emotions, relationships are the most fertile soil to use for the seeds of life.

The love of a certain earthling is the mirror of past learnings: upbringing, social background, belief system, fears within the family and education. The most important role models are the parents. I am not talking about genetics, but individuals who take the responsibility of looking after and guiding. I need to state it here that nobody is born to be a parent. Or to be the parent of the children assigned to him/her.

Affirmation

My love is unconditional

11.

Chemistry

Coming back to the idea of chemistry, like every feeling, it is produced by the mind. We carry the conditions we learned and picked up here and there; and as a result, a picture is formed about the future. This picture carries our expectations, fears, and hopes; also draws the path towards the happily ever after. And this picture is the chemistry, the interrelations of energies.

It is true that similar energies like each other. What does it mean? What are these energies?

The energy mass that you are is created by you: your thoughts, beliefs, information, and feelings. It is your data. When two persons meet they send out signals through their energy centres. After sufficient tasting, the decision is made. In the case of mixed thoughts and feelings, the tasting takes quite a while. With indecisive feelings, mixed signals are released. The initial decision is created according to the preference of the owner. If your main aspect of a relationship is sexuality, the sex centres will communicate and you make your mind up according to that signal. If it is let's say warmth and kindness, your heart centres will talk. This way you can easily figure out what the other person's intentions are. Signals sent to your sex energy centre would make it clear that the momentary approach is physical; the initial desire of communication would land in your throat centre. Naturally, conscious learning is needed to enable you to differentiate between the received and produced energy. If your mind is set on long-term relationships would be difficult to sense the signal arriving at your sex centre. But can you imagine how much time, energy and heartache could be speared by understanding the intention of the significant other? You would realize that cockiness comes from insecurity and fear, so is cheating in many cases, as an example.

By now it becomes logical that love is created in your mind by yourself. So you cannot say "I love him! I cannot help it! He abuses me but I want him!" It is only so because you do not understand chemistry, the interrelation of energies and the power of your thoughts.

Penny for your thoughts:

Affirmation

Similar energies like each other

12.

Attraction

I think some kind of explanation is needed here. I do not want to get into the subject of energies, energy centres and aura very deep, but few things need to be mentioned.

In the universe, everything is energy in the sense of physics and everything is in constant motion. As such every energy mass, like every human being, has colour, sound, taste, smell, substance, speed and frequency. I call the mentioned information pack Knowledge because it shows who you are and it is a piece of knowledge about you. It changes according to your thoughts, experiences, and understandings. It even shows the food you favour! The more exchange you have within your energy field, the faster the movement will become hence it raises the frequency of your aura. You might say now, that you did not sign up to study physics. Nevertheless, the universe works according to the laws of physics, attraction and relationship are no exceptions. So if you want to understand basic movements in life you need to acquire certain knowledge about physics. Naturally the more you know, the clearer you see. I also need to add here that blissful ignorance works very well, for those people do not want to know, they do not ask questions just follow the simple path of their ancestors. Their life is easier. However, you are not one of those people. You enrolled in this webinar! For you, there is no way back! You have to keep on learning! So when you are looking at a person from far, you only see the wrapping of the package. As wrappings, it is artificial. Usually, it has nothing to do with the content underneath. As the earthling gets nearer to you, more of his/her real nature will be revealed. The total understanding comes when your auras meet. This liaison happens between the auras. According to your level of recognition, you might experience a tinkle here and there, faster heartbeat, both could be mistakenly taken for love at first sight and special connection. They might just be! When you are frightened your heart beats faster and when you meet someone delicious your heart beat faster.

13.

Layers

I would recommend Earth Initiation from us and then carry on with the healing module.

We stated in the first webinar that similar energies like each other. That is what we call chemistry. I know it is very popular to say that opposites attract; however it is only the surface. During your existence many layers are added to your true self for protection, from attachments, mass consciousness, fashion and most of all, wanting to be somebody else. It is easy because you do not know the real you. But under all these layers, there is a wonderful human being with beauty, power, flaws, and merits, ready to conquer the world. Good people and bad people do not exist, only people. Where there is good, there is bad for they only exist together. If you do something good, it is always bad for someone. So it is good for you for that particular moment. Do not worry about it! The measure of good and bad are created by earthlings, usually males and fit their own needs and desire. Some religions put an aim up that is impossible to reach, such as be an angel! Angels are genderless spirits with no feelings. You are an earthling, with gender, feelings and a physical body. So this aim is not valid for you. Buddhism is also urging you to stay out of feelings-related events.

Also, the opposites are mirrors of the same thing. As an example, some people withdraw, become shy and introverted because they are insecure. Others will be arrogant, loud and extravert for the same reason. We take them for opposites but they only deal with the same problem differently.

Who you are attracted to, says a lot about you as a person. It is neither good nor bad. It shows the state where you are on your life's journey. Perhaps you are after someone gentle, shy and quiet, in the hope that it stays that way and you will have a harmonious relationship without big upheavals and quarrels. First of all, remember, harmony is overrated; without emotional movements, a person fades away and loses the life elixir. This case peace-making in the kitchen and bedroom will not bring solutions, boredom sets in and life becomes a routine. Routine! I know many of you consider this word manifesting the magic of relationships, but please think of it! Routine means that you need to go through the same experience over and over again! Why would anybody like that? Isn't it boring?

Apart from being a bore, this behaviour pattern is taking the essence of existence away. Remember, life is an experiencing and learning journey where you try out all of the emotions on the rainbow scale.

Do not be afraid of crying! It is a good cleansing of thoughts stuck in the throat. It doesn't mean that you are weak or unhappy as a matter of fact. It only sends the dark clouds away. These clouds are created by fear. Your fear.

And do not be afraid of laughing either! It is also a good cleansing method and puts sparkle into your eyes.

Affirmation

I invest my emotions in relationships

14.

Events to confront

Entering into a relationship should solely be your choice. With it, I am not saying that arranged marriages are bad. I think that if both of you set your minds on it, it could turn out to be the clearest road to live happily ever after. Having limited choices make your efforts stronger and easier to succeed. On the other hand, endless possibilities will present you with careless actions and neglect. The moral of the story is that you need to enter into every relationship as if it was the only possibility and it is up to you to build it and prolong it until death do us part. And I am not talking to women here! I am talking to everybody, regardless of gender, education, upbringing, social background, and religion.

To do that, emotions tarnished in previous engagements should be varnished and be ready for new adventures. This motion is only possible if you do understand that you are just as much responsible for events of the past than the other person concerned. Bear in mind that the other person was mirroring your behaviour, so you might as well figure out the thoughts you need to improve upon. You cannot, in any circumstances bring in the past, and even worse, make your new partner responsible for the happenings. Thoughts like *"I cannot open up anymore. I cannot trust women because I was cheated on by my ex."* Or *"I am off sex now because my ex wanted me every day. I hated it!"* make me wonder about the outcome of the new relationship.

Talking about an ex mistreating you in the past will strike sympathy initially but the idea always be in the background with the question: *"Why?"* It will make you damaged goods. It will also open the possibility of hurting you again.

Although we are equal, as I said, we are not the same. There are fundamental differences in understanding between the two genders. This dissimilarity derives from the brain that triggers a different view on life. Naturally, it is all related to sex. In case a female, the sexual centre is next to the hearing centre. That is why females are seduced through talking. They are taken by words. It also means that they submerge in detail. While the sexual centre of a male is near the seeing centre. They work with their eyes and look at events globally. These differences are really important. They hold the key to everything. However, I stop talking about it for now. You will have the opportunity to learn it from another book or one of my webinars.

With the motherly instinct, females appear to be far forgiving and they do like nurturing. However, it is not a gender difference. Due to the mystification and mental manipulation of motherhood for thousands of years, we have been hanging onto this *only we can do* business.

In the case of a male, this approach is a winner. They moan about the girlfriend, wife or exes and there is always someone to jump and help out. The deeper the wounds the better the treatment. There is no such health service on Earth that would do a better job. However, you have to realize that it is not couplehood but motherhood with sex.

Well, reading my words, they might sound a bit harsh. Even to me and I am used to my words. They might just be. Nevertheless, we are aiming for good and meaningful togetherness. We are aiming for learning and evolving. We are aiming for greatness.

The influence of the family and close friends need to be looked at too. Please appreciate that the members of your family are earthlings who happened to carry a few of your gens. That is all. Look at them as people, listen to them as people without giving them allowances or punish them more than you would a stranger.

Let us take on the commonly believed idea that your family would not want you to get hurt. Sure! However, they are people, they went through events and formed opinions according to their understanding. Age doesn't make anybody wiser.

Therefore you listen and make up your mind. It is your life your responsibility.

Penny for your thoughts:

Affirmation

I love myself and embrace loving

15.

Depth of Feelings

It might be difficult to understand, but I say and teach that everything is sex. Eating, drinking, shopping, working and whatever you can imagine. They all carry the Elixir of Life, the Fire, the creative power. The joy of eating something delicious, or just eating, buying a pretty dress should give you the same tinkle as sexual advances. It doesn't come to your mind because nobody said that to you and you might think it is sort of pervert or improper. However, it is a narrow-minded view of the beauty of existence. The joy of life is in everything. And in this sensual arena, the biggest junk of feelings come from human relationships.

Once again, we need to go back to the starting point, the piano. Well, there are no pianos in dancing schools any longer, but when I was at one, the piano was the place where we always started over. It means the beginning.

There is a saying that you don't choose your family. I tempt to disagree. Before coming down to Earth we make a pact of getting into the family where we can learn the most. This learning might entail a lot of arguments, emotional distress and suffering to push us into a higher state of mind and evolve. Or not. The braver and stronger survives and the weaker would succumb to the family influence. Within the family, you can see it first-hand how a romantic relationship works. Unfortunately, we rarely look at our parents as human beings. Only as providers and some kinds of servants who should follow your comfort and forget about romance or their individual lives. While you are dreaming about hot summer nights and feverish sex in your future, you would not imagine it for your parents. You look at them as the older generation and somehow you find it logical that only you have the right to that kind of enjoyment. It would be interesting to put timing to your pictures of the future. When it comes to you, you'll be fit, young and sexually active at the age of 45. In most cases your parents are younger, still, in your mind, there are old for hanky-panky. Remember back, you most probably did not see your parents kissing or cuddling very often because you might have wanted their full attention and the cuddles for yourself or they might have been ashamed of intimacy in their own home; there is always some guilt associated with parenthood and keep in mind that they learned morals and values from their ancestors. As you learn from yours. Interestingly in your picture of the future, you see only the two of you. There are no demanding children, like yourself, no electricity bill and work problems, only the blissful Nirvana. Or you might see children, one each, perfectly behaving, not disturbing your idyllic fantasy. It might be the best place to tell you to remember the golden rule if you plan to have a rewarding life: you are a lover first, secondly, you are a partner and thirdly you are a parent. I know, I know, I know! You are saying, that you want to learn, you are open-minded but this is too much! As I mentioned, you should not dismiss anything, before giving it good, deep thinking. It is very logical. If you are unhappy as a lover your relationship is doomed. Do not fool yourself! Sex is important! And if you are unhappy as a partner you are not going to be a good parent. What children need is guidance on the path, and how can you give guidance when you are lost?

Penny for your thoughts:

16.

Happiness is a state of mind

Happiness is a way of looking at life. It is a philosophy, not a momentary joy. It means that you understand that life is learning and wherever we come from, whatever we do we help each other with experiences.

Happiness is to understand that earthlings are all equal regardless. Not the same though but equal.

Happiness is to take on board that you as a human being have flaws and merits, none of which makes you a better or a lesser person.

Happiness is to understand that you are a creative part of this whole and that you are responsible for your deeds, words, and thoughts. Since we live in interrelation, I take it a step further: you are responsible for the actions of others too. It is so for every action is triggered by another action. And what we see is not what is there.

Happiness is when you have aims and able to see the core not only the surface.

Happiness is when you know that it is more than all right to be sad, angry, hurtful and joyous with all the other feelings you need to learn from. When you understand that emotions are not weaknesses.

Happiness is when you do not expect but observe.

It might sound very difficult to arrive at this stage in life but it is not. The key is equality and the understanding that every person is doing 100% of his ability at every given moment.

Translate it to relationships, there are few things I would like to talk about.

First of all, there is a question for you:

- What would you consider the meaning of happiness?

Penny for your thoughts:

17.

Two individuals

It is fashionable to say that there are two halves making one, in a relationship. However, it could be the real downfall of the 2 persons involved. This concept means that you cannot exist without the other and you put the responsibility of your life, joy, and learning on your partner. I should not say partner because in partnership there is independence. The favourable aspect of this situation is that you might have to stick together for sheer existence, and in your mind, it comes to forever. But what kind of life is there? One of you will dominate because someone needs to make decisions. If you are the one, events will lean towards your path, will or desire. However, exercising your will power 100% is not possible, because there is another earthling in the relationship and this person is not a programmed robot. Therefore you will lose some of your desires intended for togetherness and because you are so busy putting your feet down, you will not have time to pursue your personal aims. Looking at events from this point of view you will end up being a double loser. On the other hand, your partner, as an oppressed person might just say enough is enough one day and breaks free. You will be left there, by yourself, with no one to boss around and without personal prospects. I am sure you remember similar situations at work. Usually, bosses do that. Take your pride and confidence away to control you and make you do their work. Sometimes it is mistaken for good work delegation. If you have ever been in this situation, remember the feeling and do not do it to your partner.

The idea is to help each other to achieve individual goals in life.

- What are your goals, interests, and hobbies?

Penny for your thoughts:

18.

Togetherness

Another big mistake of a relationship is that people want to do everything together. The argument is that I have you now, why should I go alone? What would my friends and my family say? What will I do by myself? These are not valid questions. Your partner is not a show-monkey and if you do not know what to do with yourself at an event, I think it is time to reconsider going there.

This type of behaviour pattern limits the power of the union and that of the people involved. It also undermines the trust, the respect and weakens the sexual tie. Nobody will take on a nagger for long. It reflects mistrust and uncertainty about the relationship and your partner in it. There is a bit of naivety in this behaviour. Think about it! When you distrust your partner you are losing trust in yourself. You are afraid of not being good enough for him. You also need to note that distrust will never change into trust. Therefore the moment you encounter suspicion should be the time to give the relationship up. Otherwise, both of you will face emotional agony that would later reflect in physical illnesses, particularly that of the digestive system.

Although we live the, *happily ever after,* there are no assurances in couplehood. So you might as well trust. Yes, indiscretion could happen, and if it does, you have to confront it then. Forgiveness has to be sincere. It means that you never mention it again and you do not think about it. However, you need to figure out the cause and address it. People only stray if they miss something.

I recommend couples to take a short holiday apart from each other. It would give them time to reflect on the relationship from a distance and make an inventory of the individual goals they have. Despite the common belief, it strengthens the unity.

Penny for your thoughts:

19.

Your partner is your new family

This concept needs to be clarified. Regardless of the status of your relationship, you need to consider your partner to be your new family. It means that you do your togetherness consciously. Otherwise, there is no point in doing it at all. Ideas such as we are together only until someone better comes along is disrespectful towards yourself and the other person involved. It is a time and energy waster. It is a limbo situation where you are between two chairs and one of them is only in your mind. And you cannot look for it in real-time because you are half sitting on another one. You are tied to it. You have to free yourself, to give it up completely and then look for a better one. Also, better is a comparison. Who are you comparing to this person? Your ideal mate? The fashionable view? The requirement of your parents? You have to stop doing that. Everybody is an individual with flaws and merits. Something you need to discover.

Either way, there is no place for the opinion of the parents or other relations unless you ask for help and guidance. You need to understand that just because they are older, your parents are not necessarily better equipped to handle situations. Think about it! Others only see your connection from their point of view. Naturally, it only works if you have a place of your own. If it is not the case, you have to take everything from your parents, because it is their house. They worked for it and they have authority over the house rules. If you want your authority, you need to consider moving away and starting a new life of your own.

Relying upon the backing of your parents is not the brightest idea. It might seem comfortable at the beginning, especially if you dislike changes, but would cause a lot of headaches later. Please rethink it even if your parents insist upon that. You see, it is a change for them also. Living with children for many years usually shifts the focus of the couple to their children and they conveniently forget about couplehood. When offspring decide to leave the family unit suddenly everything would fall apart. The purpose of life and living together disappears and existence becomes meaningless. To prevent this event parents do their best to hang onto their children as long as possible. For you, it is a great example not to follow with your children. This case worsens when due to a shift the family breaks up during the upbringing of the children and one of them, usually the mother, seemingly gives up her life to look after the children. This way of reasoning would haunt the children forever. They would be held responsible for the welfare and the entertainment of the parent. However, there is something important to look at. No child on Earth consciously wanted to be born. It is the responsibility of the parents to look after them until a certain age. I will talk about parenting in a later publication.

It doesn't mean that you should not love or respect your parents. I am only saying that when you get to the stage to step to start a life of your own, then step forward and do not fall backward. Your chosen partner should be your new family and everything related to your lives has to be discussed by the two of you.

If you want to follow the way I have just given put yourself in the relationship whole-heartedly. Do not be afraid of disappointments. It is part of the learning procedure. If one of you wants to walk out, do not take it as a reflection on your value. It only shows that the two of you are not at the same place in the evolution and you need adjustments. A break-up is always the result of miscommunication or misunderstandings between the couple. It is no-one's fault because we give 100% of our capabilities at every given moment. For an outsider, every situation looks different. Friends and family would usually favour the closest to them. I am saying usually. Not always. But whatever happens, in front of others, you need to take your partner's side in any kind of dispute.

Penny for your thoughts:

20.

Respect each other

And now we have arrived at my other very important point. There should be no relationship of any kind without respect. By respecting your partner you value yourself. And do not say that I want his/her respect first and then I will reciprocate it. Life doesn't work that way. In my practice as a life coach and relationship counsellor I meet people daily who think that lining up the partner's flaws would gain them justification for disrespect. Secretly they also think, that in the end they would be valued as the better person in the relationship. They are waiting for the sentence: You deserve much better. Confusion sets in when I don't say it. Nobody deserves better. It was your choice! Why did you make that choice? Perhaps out of insecurity, fear, ignorance, outside influence; whatever pushed you towards the decision, still, it was your choice. You cannot possibly blame it on anybody! Not on your friend who introduced you, or society, because you made that choice. And do not regret it either! That was the choice you were capable of making. I do not say only this choice for a reason. Nobody is an Only! Just because the two of you cannot make it, there are many beautiful relationship prospects ahead for both persons involved.

Respect doesn't allow you to judge. And judging we do a lot nowadays. As if we created the universe and we knew it all! No, we do not. We are learning! And we are learning from each other.

Penny for your thoughts:

21.

Learn your partner

And with this thought, we arrive at my next point. We need to learn our partner. How do we learn somebody? First, we have to establish that everybody is different. You trust your partner and give him/her the benefit of the doubt. Without trust, there is no relationship. I know it is very popular to say that I am careful, I do not want to get hurt and I need proof. But if you are uncertain at the beginning, you will always have doubts no matter what your partner does. Do not forget the saying one is innocent until one is proven guilty! Instead of doubting, learn your partner. There are reasons behind his way of thinking also. He was brought up differently, he had certain experiences in the past and he might have read books on behaviour patterns and visited webinars where he was urged to keep the upper hand. And it is true for female participants too. Questions should be asked, and conversations opened.

There is a story that has been in my mind recently. You might have come across it on the internet.

There was a lady who invited a baby python into her house. It was fed and looked after very nicely so, in a few years, it developed into a beautiful giant reptile.

Over the time they spent in each other's company she became more and more attached to the oversized pet, until one day she invited it to share her bed. She stripped down to nothing and let the python curl around her while sleeping.

It all went well for a while, she was sleeping there, the giant pet was curling around her, getting closer; she thought it was a sign of bonding. One day the python stopped eating. She became very worried about the pet and took it to the vet. The doctor asked her the reason she slept with the snake. She said it kept her warm. Then the specialist examined the snake and told the owner that her friend was engaged with her, meaning fixated, and was planning to eat her.

Can you imagine? What a mismanagement of a couplehood! Sleeping with a reptile to keep her warm! She had to be a well-off person to keep, feed and look after this giant pet. And she didn't have money for heating? And naked? It is purely sexual! Mind you sleeping with any kind of pet is sexual, as sleeping with anybody would come to. Clearly, she forgot to learn and consult the other being in this relationship about the aims of their togetherness.

Well, that's what happens when the aims are not clear.

Penny for your thoughts:

Affirmation

My partner is a lesson to be learned

22.

A relationship doesn't save your life

Generally, people have the idea that a licenced relationship is Life itself and the meaning of life is to procreate. The *live happily ever after* slogan doesn't help. This thought has been chiselled into our brain by religions and the consumerist society. I am not saying that you should not aim for couplehood and children but it cannot be the goal of life.

Through life one experiences and learns. Getting married and having children are very good grounds for certain experiences. However, they are rarely adding to your character if your life circles around the family. It can greatly enrich your path and evolution. What I am saying is, do not give up yourself and your dreams. Work on them regardless. Get the best out of life and give yourself holidays without the family and children.

These are events run parallel with pursuing your personal goals. If you are lost in life and nothing goes the way you desire, a relationship, marriage, and children are not going to rescue you. Find yourself first and then share the path with someone.

Life is a theatre where different plays are on show. Since in this case, we talk about your establishment, it is axiomatic that you take the leading role in most of the plays. It is also your preference to find the best fitted and most effective genre to display. There are drama, comedy, musical and the rest to choose from. Being a conscious theatre owner you would want to give roles to your colleagues where they have the possibility to learn, open up and improve. And you all want to have fun on the road.

- What is your excuse for wanting or not desiring a relationship?

Penny for your thoughts:

23.

Stocktaking

I would suggest stocktaking to everybody at least twice a year to see the direction you are following, look at your aims and understand yourself better in the prospect of living. It needs the utmost honesty and a bit of time.

Grab four sheets of A4 size papers. Put up the headings: what I like in myself; what I dislike in myself; all my dreams I have ever had; dreams I fulfilled; on the top of the papers respectively. Start writing. You need around one month for this exercise. Every day you add and remove entries from the list if necessary. Sometimes it is not easy to admit to our flaws and could be even more difficult to write down the merits we consider having. You need to look at yourself on the outside, like your features, body, hair, and so on, and the inside, such as characteristics. It is very important that you do not discuss it with anybody. It is only for yourself, about yourself.

During the first few days, you will see the surface. But as time goes by you start remembering and finding the depth, the long-forgotten and those you pushed into the background. It is like a wardrobe: Your newly bought pullover will be your favourite. You use it, wash it and put it into your wardrobe on the top. Naturally, it will be the first one to come to mind when one is needed. The rest would fade into the past and will only be re-discovered when you decide to re-organize your clothing. I love it when I find all sorts of treasures hiding there! Don't you?

Well, about your dreams: you need to recall your childhood ideas and plans for the future as well as those you made as an adult. If you wanted to become a prima ballerina or a pop star or a baker as the matter of fact, these dreams are still in you deep down, waiting to be started on or discarded. It is a little ritual you need to do in order to get rid of unwanted dreams. Light an unscented white candle of any size, without a metallic holder. Extend your palm in front of you, and in your mind, place the dream onto your palm and say: dream of such and such, thank you very much for being with me. Now I release you into the universe. It is a necessity, for old dreams stick together and create blockages within the body.

That is what stocktaking is all about. To find hidden treasures and unwanted thoughts to discard.

I remind you again, that everybody has flaws and merits. Since you have the opposite of everything in you, the merits add up to an equal amount of flaws. Some of them are changeable and some of them are not. Let's say you are 4'9" short and you dream about being 6'2" tall. Well, I do not know any kind of advanced technology to make it happen. However certain body parts could be changed, hair dyed, contacts can change the colour of your eyes and so on. It is important to differentiate between changeable and unchangeable to take the necessary steps. My motto is:

God give me the Serenity

To accept the things

I cannot change.

Courage to change the things I can.

And wisdom always to see the difference.

I hope it becomes yours too.

It means that you need to start loving the things you cannot change and start changing those you can in the dislike category.

The same rules apply to your dreams. You either let them go or start fulfilling them.

Have a wonderful life, and I hope to see you at one of my webinars.

Live in the present!

Real joy only comes to you if you let your guards down.

The more you know, the more you enjoy

Other books from the author:

- **5 Secrets of the Matrix** – The true core of Self-development
- **Dancing with the Desertwolf** – Life, my eternal Love
- **Heavenly nourishment** – Conscious eating in 7 steps
- **The 4th Way** – Teaching the Gnostic Wisdom of AKIA Philosophy
- **Life is Yours to Win** – It All Happens in the Mind
- **The five minutes man and the girl who fell in love with mint**
- **Siblings –** As above so below
- **Siblings –** And they work together
- **Siblings –** Pandemic the story of mankind
- **Conscious togetherness –** A love affair

Thank you for leaving a review.

I hope you enjoyed the book. I know it is a bit radical for our brainwashed taste however there should be a wakeup call before we blend into oblivion forever.

Just take it as slowly as you feel comfortable. Not too comfortable though. Advancing demands a step out of the comfort zone. Otherwise, you are only chasing your own tail.

Stay safe! Have a nice day!

www.ingramcontent.com/pod-product-compliance
Lightning Source LLC
Chambersburg PA
CBHW051657040426
42446CB00009B/1181